Good Bugs

$f$or

Your Garden

written and illustrated

by

Allison Mia Starcher

Algonquin Books of Chapel Hill
1995

Published by
ALGONQUIN BOOKS OF CHAPEL HILL
Post Office Box 2225
Chapel Hill, North Carolina 27515-2225

a division of
WORKMAN PUBLISHING COMPANY, INC.
708 Broadway
New York, New York 10003

Library of Congress Cataloging-in-Publication Data

Starcher, Allison Mia.
   Good bugs for your garden / Allison Mia Starcher.
       p.   cm.
       Includes bibliographical references and index.
       ISBN 1-56512-071-X
       1. Beneficial insects.   2. Garden pests—Biological control.   I. Title.
   SF517.S88   1995
   635'.0497—dc20   94-43964
                                                                          CIP

10 9 8 7 6 5 4 3 2 1
First Edition

For my

mother

and

father

Thank you to...

Betsy Amster and
Angela Miller for
their vision,
inspiration, and
diligence.

Elisabeth Scharlatt,
Amy Gash, Julia Boss,
and everyone at Algonquin
Books for the freedom to see
my dream and the guidance
and skill to make it
a reality

Thanks to the following people
who have graciously shared
with me their knowledge,
experience and love of insects:

Anne Frodsham,
Rosser Garrison, Los Angeles County Entomologist
Jan Dietrick and Everett J. "Deke" Dietrick of Rincon-Vitova
Jim Davis of American Insectaries, Inc.
Joel Grossman, Max E. Badgley and Steve Kutcher.

Lili Singer and Phyllis Benenson,
who helped me find my
misplaced talents and
nurtured them to fruition.

And for their faith and support,
Mari and Herb Isono,
Risa and Ron Kleyweg
and all my dear friends.

Contents

Introduction

I never gave insects much thought until I began to battle a never-ending parade of snails, aphids, and caterpillars in my garden. I'd know it was spring when I would walk out into the garden to find my roses covered with aphids. As a fairly conscientious organic gardener, I just couldn't bring myself to douse my plants with chemicals. So began a quest to educate myself about the *good* bugs that either already inhabited my garden or might be persuaded to take up residence there. Like most of you, I didn't want to know everything about every bug. I just wanted to know about the beneficial ones—those whose habits help control the peskier insects that damage our plants. What did they look like? Where were they found? What did they eat? And how could I keep them happy in my garden?

Many of the insects beneficial to my own garden are ones I used to kill before, thinking, as most people do, that the only good bug is a dead bug. I was recently at a local nursery and overheard a customer asking how to kill beetles in her garden. When the salesperson asked her what type of beetle, she said, "All of them." That indiscriminate desire to rid the garden of all insects is what I hope to discourage.

A few enlightened people know that the ladybird beetle (or ladybug) is a gardener's friend, but few gardeners know that the ground beetle, which might easily be mistaken for a darkling beetle, eats caterpillars, not plants. Killing all beetles just to kill the bad beetles is a fine way to promote the proliferation of other harmful pests. If predatory and parasitoid insects didn't control other insect populations, humans would find the earth uninhabitable. Humans are, for the most part, blind to the delicate balance that nature has created around us. We either don't notice the bugs in our midst or run in terror from the ones we do see. In this book, I encourage gardeners everywhere to open their eyes to the often overlooked inhabitants of our immediate environment and appreciate how beautiful—and useful—insects can be.

Learn to Observe the Hidden Life in Your Garden

Novice and experienced gardeners alike can learn to observe closely not only their plants but also the tiny creatures living on and around them. The next time you pick some herbs for a salad or fertilize your tomatoes, move in a little closer and investigate the insects that call your plants home. I can often be found with my nose inches away from my rosebushes, watching the tiniest wasps or hover fly larvae attacking aphids. A couple of years ago, all I would have noticed were the aphids and reached for the chemical solution. Now I observe the predators, too, and wait a couple of days to see if nature (combined, perhaps, with a stiff spray from the hose) will control the situation. More often than not, it does.

This is not, however, a system to satisfy the perfectionist. Eradication of all garden pests cannot be achieved by beneficial insects alone. Integrated pest management (IPM) is a more systematic way to substantially reduce pest populations. This book's aims are more humble, leaving such complex strategies to the scientists. I offer one tool, based on common sense and old-fashioned ingenuity, that can help you to grow tomatoes and roses that are safer for your family and the environment, while also providing the opportunity to see nature at work, transforming your garden from a decorative element into a miniature, balanced ecosystem. For me, that's satisfaction enough.

The Good Old Days

Although organic gardening has recently become chic, it wasn't all that long ago that everyone used natural techniques, simply because they had no alternative. My grandmother Starcher had to be a successful gardener to feed seven children during the Great Depression. She grew a large variety of fruits and vegetables. But as my father tells it, she always made sure that their house was surrounded by flowers, too: hollyhocks, bachelor's buttons, sweet William, cosmos, snapdragons, black-eyed Susans, sunflowers, and peonies, just to name a few. So her garden was diverse, making it hospitable for all kinds of beneficial insects and harder for one type of pest to get a foothold. She grew everything without chemical pesticides or fertilizers, partly by choice and partly because she couldn't afford to do otherwise. My mother's parents ran a nursery prior to World War II, and after the war my grandfather Isono was a professional gardener. Neither my mother nor I can recall ever seeing him use any chemicals on his plants.

I now live in the house that used to be my maternal grandparents', surrounded by the trees and shrubs that my grandfather lovingly planted. Although I have a hard time taking out anything that my grandfather put in, I've succeeded in establishing my own imprint on the yard. I started as most people do, buying a few pansies to brighten up my little patch of earth—and then I found myself craving more. More color, more variety, better performance, and less damage. I've been tempted more than once to take the easy way out and use pesticides to keep my garden looking picture perfect, but instead I've followed my grandparents' example and planted a garden diverse enough to keep itself healthy. It may be more work initially, but it has saved me time in the long run.

I adore English gardens, and that's the style I've aspired to, but in truth my garden is a bit of a hodgepodge. It's chock full of flowering herbs, which not only attract lots of good bugs but also add rich fragrance and flavor to my yard and home. The odd tomato plant poking out from between perennials is a common sight in my garden, where the edible and decorative live side by side. I try to use native varieties whenever possible, but the only rule in my garden is that there are no rules. I love to experiment and hate to weed, so it's lucky for me that leaving a few weeds actually encourages a more diverse insect population.

In the back corner of my yard, behind the vegetable patch, my compost pile sits under the lemon tree. My grandfather and father started me composting as a small child and I wouldn't feel my garden was complete without the dark, rich humus the pile yields. Paired with recycling, composting reduces my garbage to almost nothing and it makes a great shelter for hard-working earthworms and ground beetles.

My garden is beautiful. It's also teeming with life—ladybird beetles, green lacewings, crab spiders, butterflies, birds, squirrels, and bees are all welcome. I wouldn't have it any other way.

Why Are Some Insects Considered Beneficial?

The creatures in this book who have earned the title "beneficial" are beneficial to humans—their behaviors help us to control insects that otherwise would feed off our gardens. In other words, they kill our enemies. Bad insects are generally plant-eating insects. They are our competition. The beneficial creatures included in this book can be divided into four categories: predators, parasitoids, pollinators, and soil builders. *Predators* such as the praying mantids and spined soldier bugs are inclined to eat every insect in sight, both good and bad. Predators such as ladybird beetles have more specific prey and are therefore unlikely to kill other good insects.

The most efficient beneficials are the *parasitoids*, creatures that derive their nourishment from the body of a host insect.

Parasitoids don't kill the host immediately but attack it by laying their eggs on, in, or near it. When the parasitoid's young hatch, they feed on the host, which dies just as the beneficial larvae reach maturity. Unlike predators, whose tastes are often indiscriminate, most parasitoids have very specific hosts. The tiny braconid wasp, for example, can kill a whole plant's worth of aphids, and trichogramma wasps are murder on tomato hornworms. By recognizing and using parasitoids in your garden, you can fight off a specific pest without endangering the lives of the many good bugs.

Also included are a few insects that don't kill other bugs. The relationship between these various insects and plants is even more complex than the relationships they have with each other. *Pollinators*, for example, are insects that plants entice into helping them reproduce. These insects are rewarded for their services with nectar and pollen from the plant. Bees are probably the most well-known and important pollinators. Plants use all sorts of crafty methods to encourage insects to visit and consequently to spread pollen from flower to flower and plant to plant. Fortunately for us gardeners, the way plants attract insects is to infuse their flowers with color and rich scent.

Lastly, there are the *soil builders*. A book about beneficial garden creatures just wouldn't be complete without mentioning earthworms. I have such good feelings toward them that I often assume they are universally prized. If, like me, you reserve a space in your heart and compost pile for the earthworm, just think of this as a reminder. However, if they inspire fear and loathing, my fervent wish is to help you recognize that they are worth their weight in gold—even if they still give you the heebie-jeebies.

To keep this book from becoming cumbersome and confusing, I have chosen to illustrate only one species per family and have labeled each drawing accordingly. For instance, there are many different types of ground beetles, and each type can vary in size, color, and shape. So keep in mind that the insects you find in your yard may not match the illustrations exactly. Use the drawings along with the accompanying written descriptions to help guide your identification.

The first five chapters of this book illustrate insects, the class of arthropods that have six legs, three body parts, and either one or two sets of wings as adults. The last chapter is a miscellany of other creatures such as spiders (from the arachnida class) and earthworms, which are essential elements in the garden.

How Insects Develop

Insect development, or metamorphosis, takes place in two ways. Some insects, such as the true bugs, go through a gradual metamorphosis, changing in size but not very much in appearance. Others, such as flies and beetles, go through a complete metamorphosis, changing form three times between the immature and adult stages.

Species that go through gradual metamorphosis usually eat the same food throughout the various stages of their life.

Those that go through complete metamorphosis often have different diets at different stages. Many insects eat only plants when they are in the larval stage. For example, butterflies and moths eat pollen and nectar as adults. It's their larvae—caterpillars—that do all the damage in your garden. By the same token, many beneficial insects are most useful to the gardener at the larval stage, when they live to eat. I used to think that hover fly maggots were tiny caterpillars eating my rosebuds and I would pinch them off along with the aphids that surrounded them. I felt terrible when I learned that they were eating the aphids, not the plants, and that I had been sabotaging the very thing I wanted to encourage. We all know what adult ladybird beetles look like, but how many gardeners know that ladybird beetles' larvae look like little black alligators? Therefore, I have included not only illustrations of the adult stage of each insect but often drawings of eggs and larvae when helpful (sometimes these early stages are underground or too small to detect).

How to Encourage Beneficial Bugs to Come to Your Garden

Pests flourish in what scientists like to call a monoculture: in other words, a garden with a single type of plant or a farm with only one crop and no weeds. Therefore, as my grandmother knew, the more diverse the plant life in your garden, the less likely a specific pest will be able to establish itself. You can also encourage native beneficial insects to live in your garden by providing an inviting habitat.

Many of the insects described in this book feed on pollen and nectar. Because the hybridized bedding plants found in nurseries are bred to be beautiful to humans, they have lost some of the characteristics that make them attractive to insects. Flowering herbs and wildflowers are a better source of nectar and will attract a wide variety of insects. Here are some suggested plants that produce lots of nectar and pollen to attract good bugs:

Alfalfa
Angelica
Baby-Blue-Eyes
Baby's Breath
Buckwheat
Caraway
Carrot
Clover (sweet, white, yellow, and crimson)
Coriander (Cilantro)
Cosmos (White Sensation)
Dill
Feverfew
Goldenrod
Lavender
Lemon Balm

Lovage
Marigold (Lemon Gem)
Mustard
Nasturtiums
Parsley
Queen Anne's Lace
Rose-scented Geraniums
Spearmint
Sunflowers
Sweet Alyssum
Sweet Fennel
Tansy
Thyme
White Sage . . .
. . . and any wildflowers native to your region

Note that some of these plants may become invasive if allowed to reseed. You may want to plant them on the periphery of your garden or stick to ones that don't take up too much room.

Spearmint should be planted in pots, as it will, without a doubt, take over your garden if given the chance.

I scatter these plants throughout my garden in addition to having a section specifically for herbs. Moisture of some kind is also necessary—anything from a dish filled with pebbles and water to a fishpond will do the job. Also important is shelter from wind, rain, and sun. I like to place small boards in unobtrusive spots between plants or use rocks or driftwood to create borders. I am also careful to maintain perennial plants that can serve as a fairly permanent refuge for insects.

It almost goes without saying that the broad use of insecticides is to be avoided. If you find it necessary to use pesticides, use them sparingly, only where needed, and in their least toxic form. Always remember that the complete eradication of pests is not a realistic goal, nor is it necessarily a desirable one. Don't worry if you notice that a few pests are still hanging around. If you want beneficial insects to stay in your garden, they will need something to eat. After all, if *yours* is too pest free, they might as well head over to your neighbor's garden!

Damselflies,
Dragonflies
and
Praying Mantids

Damselflies

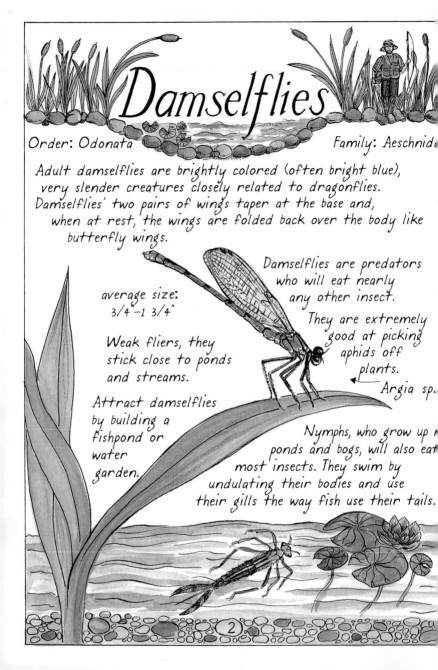

Order: Odonata   Family: Aeschnidae

Adult damselflies are brightly colored (often bright blue),
very slender creatures closely related to dragonflies.
Damselflies' two pairs of wings taper at the base and,
   when at rest, the wings are folded back over the body like
      butterfly wings.

average size:
3/4 – 1 3/4"

Weak fliers, they
stick close to ponds
and streams.

Attract damselflies
by building a
fishpond or
water
garden.

Damselflies are predators
who will eat nearly
any other insect.

They are extremely
good at picking
aphids off
plants.

Argia sp.

Nymphs, who grow up in
ponds and bogs, will also eat
most insects. They swim by
undulating their bodies and use
their gills the way fish use their tails.

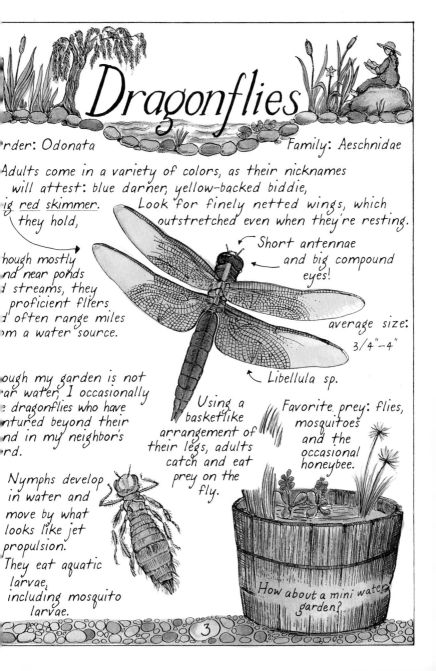

Dragonflies

Order: Odonata   Family: Aeschnidae

Adults come in a variety of colors, as their nicknames
will attest: blue darner, yellow-backed biddie,
big red skimmer.
they hold,

Look for finely netted wings, which
outstretched even when they're resting.

Short antennae
and big compound
eyes!

though mostly
and near ponds
and streams, they
proficient fliers
and often range miles
from a water source.

average size:
3/4"-4"

Libellula sp.

though my garden is not
near water, I occasionally
see dragonflies who have
ventured beyond their
and in my neighbor's
yard.

Using a
basketlike
arrangement of
their legs, adults
catch and eat
prey on the
fly.

Favorite prey: flies,
mosquitoes
and the
occasional
honeybee.

Nymphs develop
in water and
move by what
looks like jet
propulsion.
They eat aquatic
larvae,
including mosquito
larvae.

How about a mini water
garden?

Praying Mantids

Order: *Mantodea*   Family: *Mantidae*

Bright green to brownish-gray in color, praying mantids are the only insects who can look over their shoulder. Lucky for them their prey can't, as mantids usually sit motionless on plants with forelegs upraised, waiting for insects to come to them.

They will eat just about anything, which means they are just as likely to eat a leafhopper as a honeybee.

The smaller the mantid, the smaller the prey it hunts.

Mantids are well equipped for camouflage. I have been tricked more than once by their twiggy, leaflike appearance.

Look for them on plants where insect populations thrive.

average size: 3/4"–5"

They can be found in mostly warm regions throughout the world.

← Eggs are laid in cases, which can be bought at your local nursery.

200 eggs inside.

Newly hatched nymphs are such voracious eaters they have been known to eat each other!

4

The True Bugs
and
the Thrips

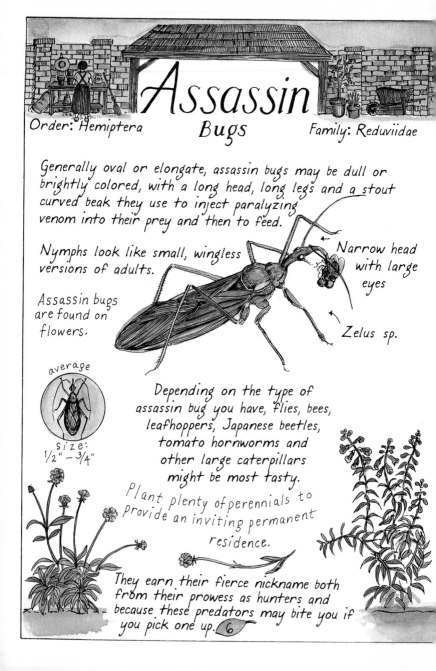

Assassin Bugs

Order: Hemiptera

Family: Reduviidae

Generally oval or elongate, assassin bugs may be dull or brightly colored, with a long head, long legs and a stout curved beak they use to inject paralyzing venom into their prey and then to feed.

Nymphs look like small, wingless versions of adults.

Assassin bugs are found on flowers.

Narrow head with large eyes

Zelus sp.

average

size:
1/2" – 3/4"

Depending on the type of assassin bug you have, flies, bees, leafhoppers, Japanese beetles, tomato hornworms and other large caterpillars might be most tasty.

Plant plenty of perennials to provide an inviting permanent residence.

They earn their fierce nickname both from their prowess as hunters and because these predators may bite you if you pick one up. 6

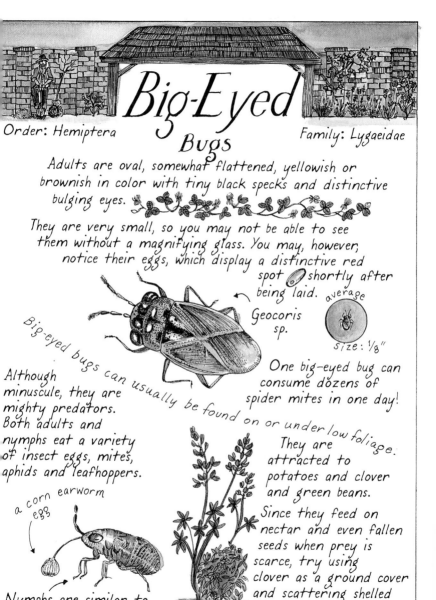

Big-Eyed Bugs

Order: Hemiptera

Family: Lygaeidae

Adults are oval, somewhat flattened, yellowish or brownish in color with tiny black specks and distinctive bulging eyes.

They are very small, so you may not be able to see them without a magnifying glass. You may, however, notice their eggs, which display a distinctive red spot shortly after being laid.

Geocoris sp.

average

size: 1/8"

Big-eyed bugs can usually be found on or under low foliage.

Although minuscule, they are mighty predators. Both adults and nymphs eat a variety of insect eggs, mites, aphids and leafhoppers.

One big-eyed bug can consume dozens of spider mites in one day!

They are attracted to potatoes and clover and green beans.

Since they feed on nectar and even fallen seeds when prey is scarce, try using clover as a ground cover and scattering shelled sunflower seeds beneath plants.

a corn earworm egg

Nymphs are similar to adults in appearance but are wingless.

7

Damsel Bugs

Order: Hemiptera

Family: Nabidae

Adults have long, thin bodies with curved, needlelike beaks. Usually dull brown or straw colored, they resemble harmful bugs, but their heads are narrower than most species that feed on plants.

Adults and nymphs prey on insects such as aphids, small caterpillars, thrips, leaf-hoppers, treehoppers and other soft-bodied insects.

Nabis sp.

The nymphs are smaller, wingless versions of adults.

They are found on low vegetation, wherever there are small insects.

After finishing a meal, they use their two front legs to wash their beaks and threadlike antennae.

average

size: ½" - ¾"

They are partial to clover. I have also seen them on the lower leaves of my tomato plants, sucking the juice out of aphid after aphid.

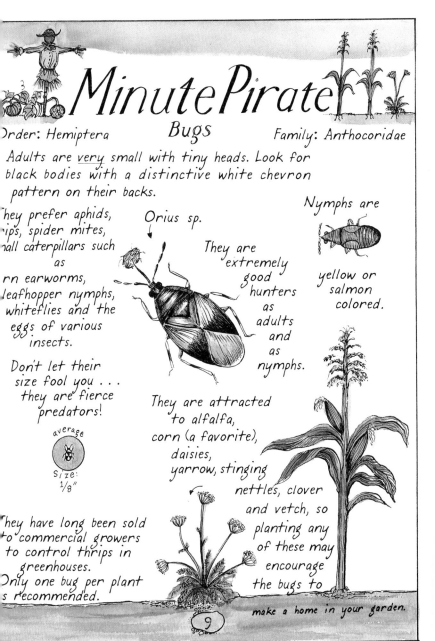

Minute Pirate Bugs

Order: Hemiptera   **Family:** Anthocoridae

Adults are <u>very</u> small with tiny heads. Look for black bodies with a distinctive white chevron pattern on their backs.

They prefer aphids, thrips, spider mites, small caterpillars such as corn earworms, leafhopper nymphs, whiteflies and the eggs of various insects.

Don't let their size fool you . . . they are fierce predators!

Orius sp.

They are extremely good hunters as adults and as nymphs.

Nymphs are yellow or salmon colored.

average Size: 1/8"

They are attracted to alfalfa, corn (a favorite), daisies, yarrow, stinging nettles, clover and vetch, so planting any of these may encourage the bugs to make a home in your garden.

They have long been sold to commercial growers to control thrips in greenhouses. Only one bug per plant is recommended.

9

Spined Soldier Bugs

Order: Hemiptera

Family: Pentatomidae

The adult is shield shaped, yellow to brown with black speckles and pointed shoulders.

The nymphs are wingless, smaller and more oval shaped than adults—usually red, orange, cream or black. Spined soldier bugs appear in crop fields and gardens on cultivated and wild species of plants.

They like to stab their prey, paralyze them by injection and then suck their body fluids.

Podisus sp.

They have been known to eat their own young.

Distinctive black line on the top of each wing

average

Size: 3/8"–1/2"

To attract, be sure to supply a permanent perennial bed for year-round shelter!

Favorite prey: caterpillars, cabbage loopers, sawfly larvae, grubs of leaf beetles, Mexican bean beetles and Colorado potato beetles.

Although for the most part beneficial, these bugs are predators and do prey on other good insects such as ladybird beetles.

Predacious Thrips

Order: Thysanoptera   Family: Thripidae

Bad thrips eat plants; good thrips, such as six-spotted thrips, banded-wing thrips and black hunter thrips, eat other bugs.

average size: 1/20"

They are especially fond of spider mite eggs and nymphs, aphids, other thrips and the eggs of corn earworms, peach borers, whiteflies, leaf miner flies and scale insects.

Extremely small, they are virtually invisible to the naked eye. Often their presence can be detected by the trail of spider mite bodies left in their wake.

Scolothrips sp.

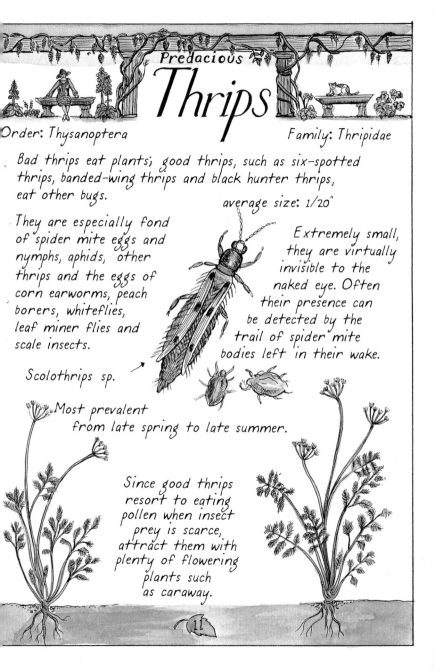

Most prevalent from late spring to late summer.

Since good thrips resort to eating pollen when insect prey is scarce, attract them with plenty of flowering plants such as caraway.

Lacewinged Insects and Beetles

Ant Lions

Order: Neuroptera

Family: Myrmeleontidae

Adults may resemble damselflies but their antennae are longer and blunter at the ends. They have long, thin bodies and veiny, transparent wings.

Ant lions are predacious as adults (they eat small insects) and as larvae (they eat ants and small insects).

They also eat ticks.

They are weak fliers.

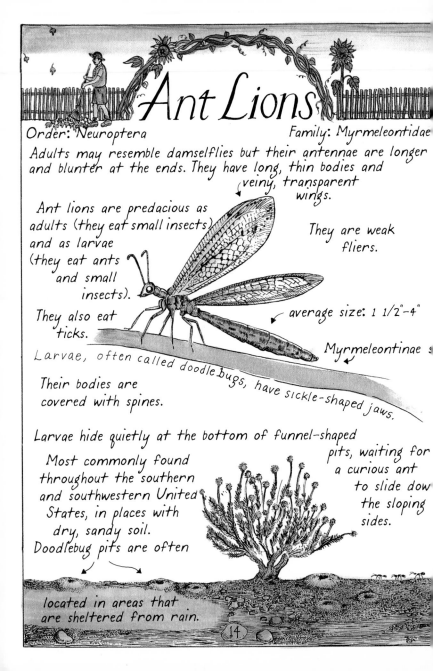

average size: 1 1/2"-4"

Myrmeleontinae s

Larvae, often called doodlebugs, have sickle-shaped jaws.

Their bodies are covered with spines.

Larvae hide quietly at the bottom of funnel-shaped pits, waiting for a curious ant to slide down the sloping sides.

Most commonly found throughout the southern and southwestern United States, in places with dry, sandy soil. Doodlebug pits are often located in areas that are sheltered from rain.

Brown
Lacewings

Order: Neuroptera   Family: Hemerobiidae

Adult brown lacewings have brown wings with a
pattern that differs from that of their kin, the
green lacewings. Brown lacewings lay their eggs
directly on leaves instead of on long filaments.

They are much
smaller than
ant lions and
green lacewings.

They are often found
near or in woods,
forests and
fields.

Predacious
as adults
as well as
larvae.

Hewerobius sp.

Larvae are called aphid wolves although they
eat a variety of other insects besides aphids.
Some eat mealybugs, nymphs of scale insects and
other soft-bodied insects.

average

size:
3/8"–5/8"

To camouflage themselves,
the spindle-shaped larvae
often carry debris (sometimes
the remains of past meals)
on their backs. This allows
them to sneak up on prey
and at the same time
avoid becoming bird food!
It has also given rise to

another apt
nickname
for the larvae:
trash carriers.

15

Green Lacewings

Order: Neuroptera   **Family: Chrysopidae**

Adults are bright green, fragile, with small heads and beautiful lacy wings. Some species have large golden eyes.

As adults, only some species of lacewings feed on insects, but their larvae are always extremely voracious predators.

Chrysopa sp.

Usually found amongst weeds and grass or on the leaves of trees and shrubs.

To encourage them to stay, grow nectar-producing plants such as angelica, corn and sunflowers, and allow for some flowering weeds

Larvae are spindle shaped, yellow to pink-brown, with curved mandibles used to impale aphids and other soft-bodied insects and to suck them dry. Hence their name: aphid lions.

The alligator-shaped larvae look like pests but they're not.

These delicate creatures are readily available from commercial sources and have a rather good reputation for sticking around in your garden.

I always find them on my scented geraniums.

Pale-green to gray eggs are laid atop long slender stalks. This helps avoid cannibalism amongst the newly hatched, extremely hungry larvae.

average

size: ½" – ¾"

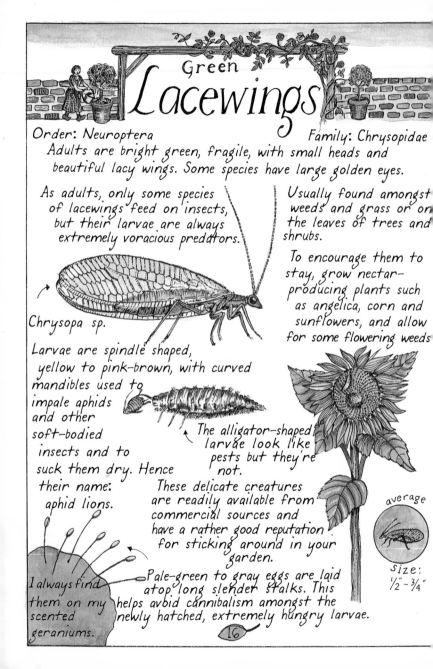

16

Ground Beetles

Order: Coleoptera   Family: Carabidae

These large blue-black or dark-brown beetles, sometimes with a bronze or green metallic sheen, are fast moving and have large, strong jaws.

The long, thin larvae, which live underground, are cream, dark brown or black.

They feed on other ground-inhabiting larvae and insect eggs.

Ground beetles are commonly found in gardens, crop fields and woods. Look for them hiding under rocks and boards. average size: 1/8"–1"

Calasoma sp.

When disturbed they may give off a fetid odor!

To attract these predators,

lay down a stone path...

plant white clover as a ground cover...

... or build a compost pile

... for them to hide under during the day.

They can live 2 to 3 years.

night hunters, they are partial to cutworms, gypsy moth larvae, and root maggots.

snails,

slugs,

A ground beetle larvae

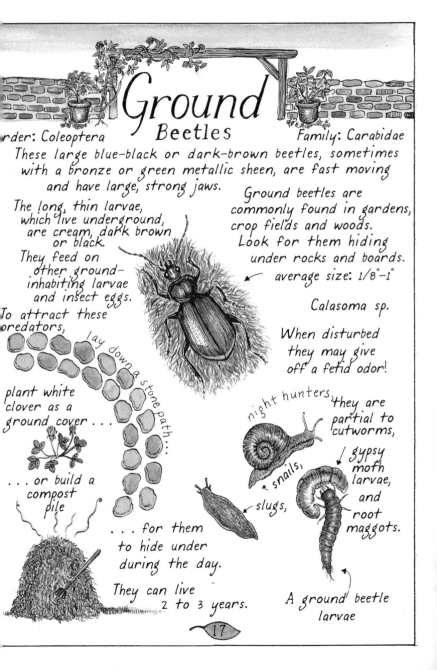

Ladybird
Beetles

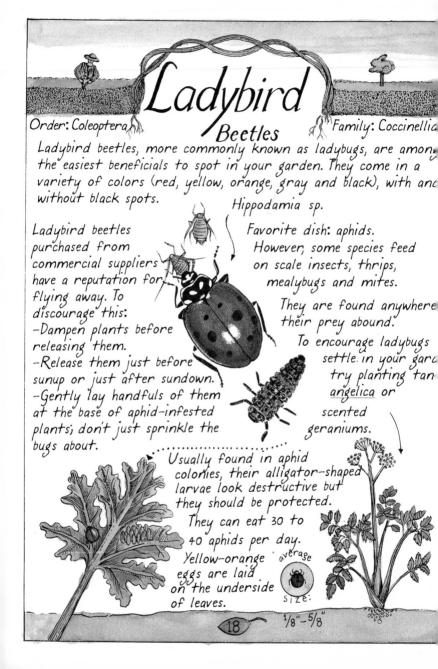

Order: Coleoptera   Family: Coccinellia

Ladybird beetles, more commonly known as ladybugs, are among the easiest beneficials to spot in your garden. They come in a variety of colors (red, yellow, orange, gray and black), with and without black spots.

Hippodamia sp.

Ladybird beetles purchased from commercial suppliers have a reputation for flying away. To discourage this:
−Dampen plants before releasing them.
−Release them just before sunup or just after sundown.
−Gently lay handfuls of them at the base of aphid-infested plants; don't just sprinkle the bugs about.

Favorite dish: aphids. However, some species feed on scale insects, thrips, mealybugs and mites.

They are found anywhere their prey abound.

To encourage ladybugs settle in your garden try planting tansy, angelica or scented geraniums.

Usually found in aphid colonies, their alligator-shaped larvae look destructive but they should be protected.

They can eat 30 to 40 aphids per day.

Yellow-orange eggs are laid on the underside of leaves.

average

size: ⅛"−⅝"

18

Mealybug
Destroyers

Order: Coleoptera   Family: Coccinellidae

Adult mealybug destroyers, sometimes called crypts (short for _Cryptolaemus montrouzieri_, their scientific name), look like black ladybird beetles with orange-red heads.

average
size: 1/8 "

Although adult mealybug destroyers will eat certain stages of scale insects and the occasional aphid, the accurately named mealybug destroyers are partial to mealybugs.

Larvae resemble monstrous mealybugs mainly because, like their prey, they produce a white cottony wax that covers and protects them from ants. This body cover also helps the larvae to infiltrate mealybug colonies.

They are present in areas without harsh winters but can be purchased commercially in other areas for use during warmer months and in greenhouses.

Ants love to eat the honeydew produced by mealybugs, so they protect them by attacking predators such as the mealybug destroyer. Using barriers or traps to control ants will help the crypts do their job.

19

Rove Beetles

Order: Coleoptera   Family: Staphylinidae

A very diverse family, usually black or brown in color with short antennae, rove beetles look a bit like earwigs (common garden pests). But their threatening pincers are their jaws not their tails—and rove beetles eat insects, not plants.

Most rove beetles and their larvae prey on mites, aphids, springtails and nematodes, as well as fly eggs and maggots.

Aleochara sp.

Elytra (wing covers) are characteristically short.

There are close to 3,000 species in North America.

To keep these valuable insects happy, maintain a permanent refuge such as a perennial bed, mulch or a stone path.

Rove beetles are usually found on fungi or flowers or under bark or leaf litter. They are common in compost piles.

average

Size: 1/16" – 3/4"

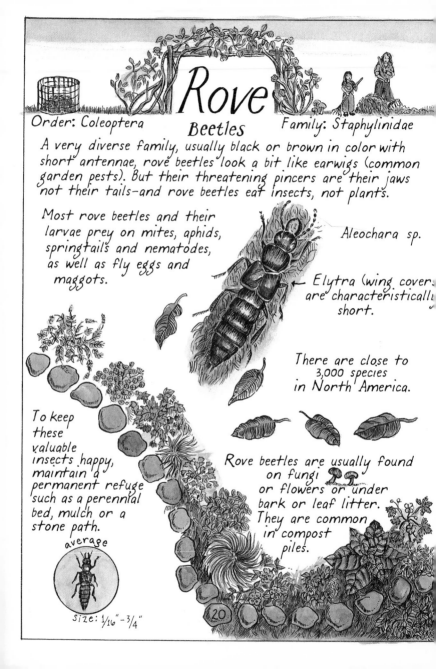

20

Tiger Beetles

Order: Coleoptera   Family: Cicindelidae

These ferocious predators vary in color from bronze to blue, green or purple, usually with a metallic sheen. They have long legs and are extremely fast runners. Many species are proficient fliers.

Over 100 species can be found throughout North America.

They prey on ants, flies, small beetles, caterpillars, aphids and grasshoppers, to name a few.

average

size: 1/2" - 3/4"

From early spring until fall, they can be found basking in the sun along roads, paths or beaches, in bare sandy spots.

Cicindela sp.

Tiger beetles have a tendency to swarm around lights, so turn off outdoor lighting to keep them working in your garden.

Be sure to include some permanent plantings so that the beetle population isn't disturbed year after year.

Chances are you won't observe many of these in your garden— they run too fast.

Larvae are S-shaped with a humpback. Strong hooks on their abdomen anchor the larvae in the soil while they seize prey in their jaws. The prey are then dragged back to the burrow and eaten.

Whitefly Predatory Beetles

Order: Coleoptera   Family: Coccinellidae

It's a shame there's not a more "user-friendly" name for this decidedly "user-friendly" bug. A close relation to ladybugs, they look like tiny, shiny black beads.

They are found where there are high concentrations of whiteflies, which adults and larvae consume at all stages of development.

Delphastus sp.

The males have brown heads.

Favorite prey: sweet potato whitefly

They may turn to eating spider mites when they run out of whiteflies.

Adults can eat several hundred whiteflies per day!

The larvae can consume about a thousand whitefly eggs before pupating.

I've tried them on my irises and they are reproducing and eating.

Results are not immediate, but each generation of these predatory beetles is 50 to 100 times more numerous than the one before, so eventually you <u>will</u> have fewer whiteflies.

average

size:
1/16"

22

Bees
and
Wasps

Bumble
Bees

Order: Hymenoptera   Family: Apidae

These highly social animals gather pollen on their hairy bodies and hind legs, cross-pollinating as they travel from flower to flower. Like all bees, bumblebees have 2 pairs of wings.

average size:
1/4"–1 1/4"

Provide them with plenty of pollen-producing plants.

More active early and late in the day than other bees, bumblebees are common everywhere except deserts.

In my yard they especially like passionflower vines, lavender and butterfly bush.

Unlike short-tongued bees (such as honeybees), bumblebees are able to pollinate clover and alfalfa.

Bombus sp.

Because bumblebees are such good pollinators, they are used in greenhouses to help grow melons and tomatoes.

Bumblebee colonies are annual, with the fertilized queen surviving the winter months and starting a new colony in the spring.

These bees nest in or on the ground. Their grublike larvae eat pollen or honey.

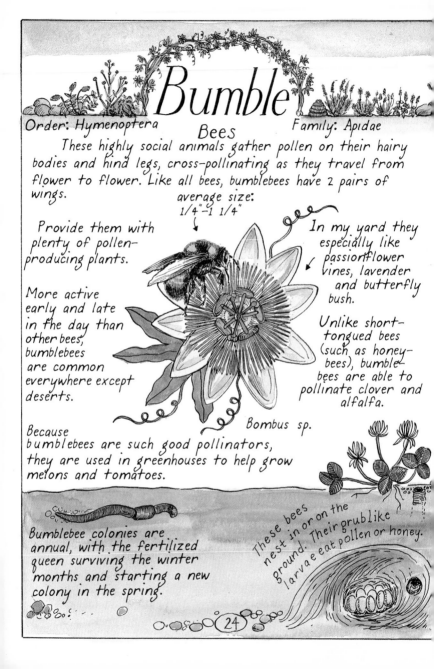

Honey Bees

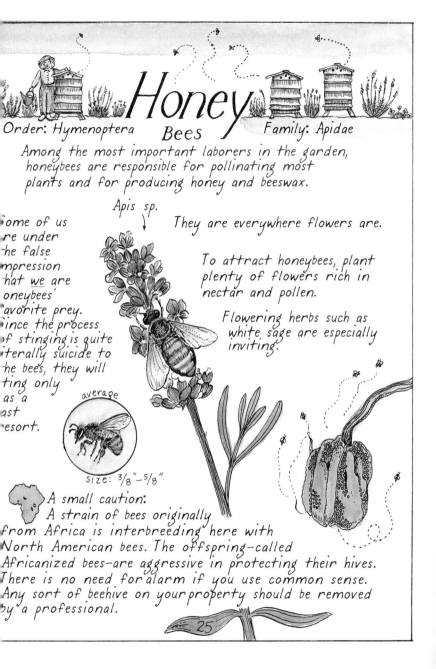

Order: Hymenoptera   **Family: Apidae**

Among the most important laborers in the garden, honeybees are responsible for pollinating most plants and for producing honey and beeswax.

Apis sp.

They are everywhere flowers are.

Some of us are under the false impression that _we_ are honeybees' favorite prey. Since the process of stinging is quite literally suicide to the bees, they will sting only as a last resort.

To attract honeybees, plant plenty of flowers rich in nectar and pollen.

Flowering herbs such as white sage are especially inviting.

average

size: 3/8" – 5/8"

A small caution:
A strain of bees originally from Africa is interbreeding here with North American bees. The offspring—called Africanized bees—are aggressive in protecting their hives. There is no need for alarm if you use common sense. Any sort of beehive on your property should be removed by a professional.

25

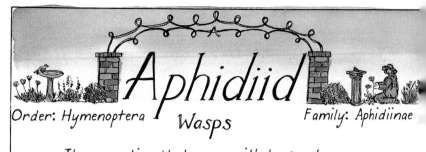

Aphidiid Wasps

Order: Hymenoptera
Family: Aphidiinae

These are tiny black wasps with long antennae.

Aphidiid wasps have one specific host, aphids. The females lay their eggs inside the aphid, where the larvae then hatch and feed on the aphid, eventually killing it.

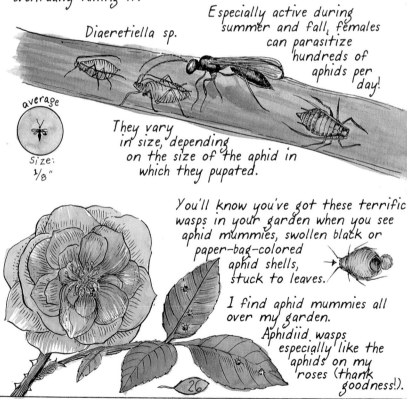

Diaeretiella sp.

Especially active during summer and fall, females can parasitize hundreds of aphids per day!

average

Size: 1/8"

They vary in size, depending on the size of the aphid in which they pupated.

You'll know you've got these terrific wasps in your garden when you see aphid mummies, swollen black or paper-bag-colored aphid shells, stuck to leaves.

I find aphid mummies all over my garden. Aphidiid wasps especially like the aphids on my roses (thank goodness!).

26

Braconid Wasps

Order: Hymenoptera

Family: Braconidae

These tiny black or brown wasps are extremely valuable. Many species are used for agricultural pest control.

Apanteles sp.

Adults feed on pollen, so . . .

They are quite common throughout North America and can be found anywhere their prey abound.

Many braconids resemble flying ants.

average

size: 1/10" - 1/2"

. . . plant some early bulbs such as crocuses or freesia to sustain the wasps early in the season and also grow nectar plants with small flowers such as sweet alyssum or wild carrot to attract them year-round.

Depending on the species, braconid hosts include tomato hornworms, armyworms, cabbageworms, codling moths, gypsy moths and other insect pupae and adults.

Since the adults are small and quite difficult to identify, look for cocoons stuck to the host caterpillar's back.

A parasitized tomato hornworm

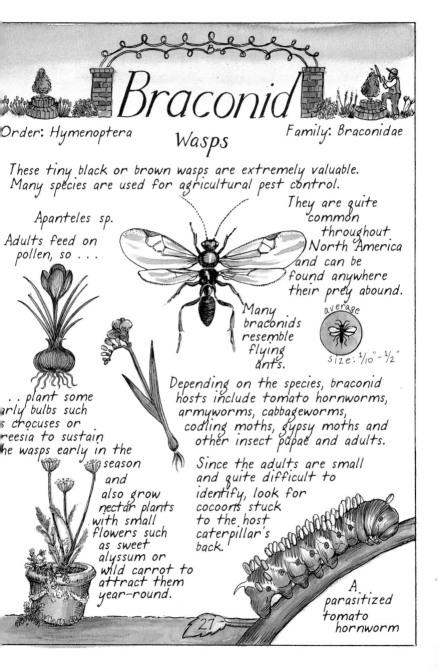

27

Encarsia
Formosa

Order: Hymenoptera   Family: Aphelinida

Adults are very tiny wasps with black heads and black thoraxes and yellow abdomens.

Adults prey on greenhouse whiteflies and sweet potato whitef

They have been used for 60 years to control whiteflies.

You can tell if whiteflies have wasp pupae inside because they turn black or brown instead of pale yellow.

They lay one egg inside an immature whitefly. As the egg grows, it kills its host. The matur wasp cuts a round hole and escapes.

The adult wasps actually feed on young whiteflies, so Encarsia wasps are predators and parasitoids.

average

size: 1/25"

Though not native to North America, these wasps are sold commercially for use in greenhouses or for outdoor use in warm areas. They are not typically hardy.

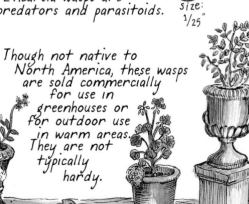

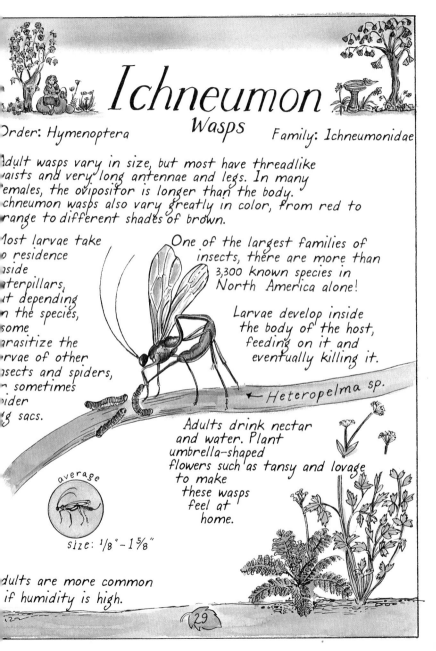

Ichneumon
Wasps

Order: Hymenoptera

Family: Ichneumonidae

Adult wasps vary in size, but most have threadlike waists and very long antennae and legs. In many females, the ovipositor is longer than the body. Ichneumon wasps also vary greatly in color, from red to orange to different shades of brown.

Most larvae take up residence inside caterpillars, but depending on the species, some parasitize the larvae of other insects and spiders, an sometimes spider egg sacs.

One of the largest families of insects, there are more than 3,300 known species in North America alone!

Larvae develop inside the body of the host, feeding on it and eventually killing it.

← Heteropelma sp.

Adults drink nectar and water. Plant umbrella-shaped flowers such as tansy and lovage to make these wasps feel at home.

average

size: 1/8" - 1 5/8"

Adults are more common if humidity is high.

Trichogramma
Wasps

Order: Hymenoptera   Family: Trichogrammatidae

These tiny, stout-bodied wasps range in color from yellow to orange to dark brown, with bright-red eyes.

All species in this family are parasitoids of the eggs of other insects. They destroy the eggs of fruitworms, hornworms, loopers, cabbageworms and others, effectively stopping them before they devour your plants.

4 or 5 will fit on the head of a pin!

average

Size: 1/50"

Wasp egg is laid on host egg

Adults feed on insect eggs, nectar, pollen and honeydew.

Parasitized eggs often turn black.

Provide a variety of plants, including flowering herbs such as caraway and fennel, tansy and Queen Anne's lace, so adults can eat the pollen.

There are several different strains of trichogramma wasps. Because each enjoys a particular climate and host, if you are purchasing from a retail source, make sure you are buying the right wasps for your pest problem.

Flies

Aphid Midges

Order: Diptera   **Family:** Cecidomyiidae

Adults are mosquitolike flies with long legs and delicate, thin bodies.

This fly is one of the most versatile insects, useful indoors for houseplants and greenhouses and outdoors in home gardens and commercial orchards.

Aphid midges are more apt to stay in your garden than ladybird beetles and are not prone to cannibalism like lacewings.

The adults survive on honeydew, pollen and nectar, so provide a variety of flowering plants such as dill, mustard and thyme.

Adults lay eggs at night.

Aphidoletes sp.

Tiny, bright-orange maggots feed on more than 60 species of aphids.

Because the aphid midge pupates in the soil, always include some perennials and a layer of mulch so the soil will not be disturbed. They are happiest in gardens where there is moisture and protection from wind.

I have aphid midge larvae all over my roses in the middle of aphid colonies.

average

Size: 1/10"

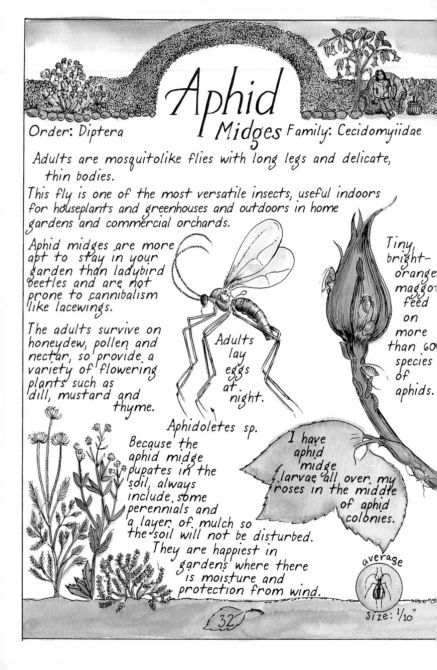

Hover
Flies

Order: Diptera   Family: Syrphidae

Adults resemble bees and wasps because of their yellow-and-black or black-and-white striped bodies, but they have only one pair of wings and they don't sting. Hover flies are sometimes called syrphid flies.

Also known as flower flies, their nicknames come from their <u>hovering</u> flight above <u>flowers</u>.

average

size:
1/2"-5/8"

Though adult flies are not predacious, they are beneficial as one of the garden's most proficient pollinators.

The hover fly's sluglike maggots are often found in aphid colonies.

Syrphus sp.

Distinctive "false" vein

Since adult hover flies need pollen to reproduce, it's important to include plenty of nectar-rich flowers in your garden. I always find them hovering over my feverfew, Italian parsley and coreopsis.

Hover fly maggots can consume aphids at a rate of one per minute for an extended period of time.

Hover flies lay their eggs singly among groups of aphids.

I see them on my rosebushes.

33

Robber
Flies

Order: Diptera

Family: Asilidae

Some robber flies are stout, resembling bumblebees; most are relatively slender and look more like damselflies.

Voracious predators, robber flies are rarely discouraged by other insects' natural defenses.

They catch flies, bees, beetles and grasshoppers by dropping down on them from above.

Efferia sp.

Very strong legs hold prey tightly

~Almost all have bearded faces with heads that appear hollowed between their bulging eyes.

average

size:
$\frac{1}{5}$" – $1\frac{1}{4}$"

Robber fly maggots are long and cylindrical, tapered at both ends.

They are usually found in meadows and are common worldwide.

Maggots live in soil or decaying wood and feed for the most part on beetle larvae.

Tachinid Flies

Order: Diptera

Family: Tachinidae

These large flies are terrific against caterpillars. Adults are identifiable by lots of coarse bristles covering their abdomens. They resemble houseflies but are usually mottled black, grayish or brownish instead of brightly colored.

average

size:
1/8" - 1/2"

To attract, you could plant . . .

tansy, spearmint or dill.

Archytas sp.

Adults feed on nectar and can often be found near flowers.

Tachinid flies prey on a variety of insects, including caterpillars, beetles, sawflies, borers and green stink bugs, to name a few.

Don't kill caterpillars with white eggs stuck to them. They will help you produce more flies.

There are hundreds of species throughout North America.

Females lay eggs on the bodies of hosts or on plants to be ingested by the host. The larvae mature inside the unsuspecting host insect, eventually killing it.

the fall armyworm is a common host.

The fully grown larvae then drop from the host and pupate in the soil.

Spiders, Mites
and
Other Helpful
Creatures

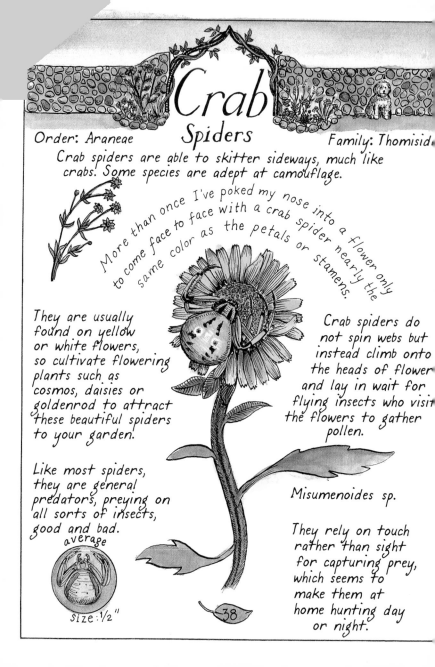

Crab
Spiders

Order: Araneae

Family: Thomisidæ

Crab spiders are able to skitter sideways, much like crabs. Some species are adept at camouflage.

More than once I've poked my nose into a flower only to come face to face with a crab spider nearly the same color as the petals or stamens.

They are usually found on yellow or white flowers, so cultivate flowering plants such as cosmos, daisies or goldenrod to attract these beautiful spiders to your garden.

Like most spiders, they are general predators, preying on all sorts of insects, good and bad.

average

size: ½"

Crab spiders do not spin webs but instead climb onto the heads of flowers and lay in wait for flying insects who visit the flowers to gather pollen.

Misumenoides sp.

They rely on touch rather than sight for capturing prey, which seems to make them at home hunting day or night.

38

Green Lynx *Spiders*

Order: Araneae

Family: Oxyopidae

These transparent, bright-green spiders have small red spots and a patch of red between their eyes.

Their abdomens usually come to a point. They eat a wide variety of insects.

Peucetia sp.

average

size: 3/4"

These spiders never make webs and do most of their hunting during the day.

3 chevronlike markings on back

Extremely agile, they are especially good at leaping with precision.

They often sit back on their hind legs with front legs raised.

To attract, plant wild buckwheat. Egg sacs can often be found tied to this plant's yellowish flowers.

They are found in the southern United States from coast to coast and in Mexico, in fields and woods, especially on tall grasses, low bushes, herbs and flower heads.

39

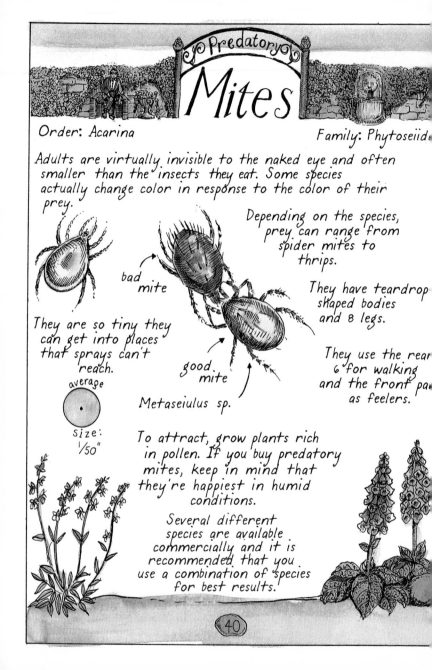

Predatory Mites

Order: Acarina

Family: Phytoseiidae

Adults are virtually invisible to the naked eye and often smaller than the insects they eat. Some species actually change color in response to the color of their prey.

Depending on the species, prey can range from spider mites to thrips.

bad mite

They have teardrop shaped bodies and 8 legs.

good mite

Metaseiulus sp.

They are so tiny they can get into places that sprays can't reach.

average

size: 1/50"

They use the rear 6 for walking and the front pair as feelers.

To attract, grow plants rich in pollen. If you buy predatory mites, keep in mind that they're happiest in humid conditions.

Several different species are available commercially and it is recommended that you use a combination of species for best results.

Decollate Snails

Order: Molluska   Family: Achatinidae

Chances are you've never thought about buying snails, but these actually eat the pesty, common brown garden snail. They look like stretched-out garden snails.

Night hunters, they feed on the eggs and flesh of small to medium-size, brown garden snails and hide during the day.

Rumina sp.

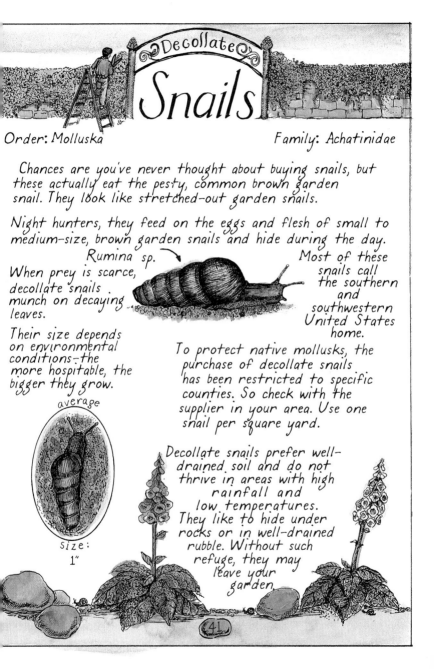

When prey is scarce, decollate snails munch on decaying leaves.

Their size depends on environmental conditions—the more hospitable, the bigger they grow.

average

size: 1"

Most of these snails call the southern and southwestern United States home.

To protect native mollusks, the purchase of decollate snails has been restricted to specific counties. So check with the supplier in your area. Use one snail per square yard.

Decollate snails prefer well-drained soil and do not thrive in areas with high rainfall and low temperatures. They like to hide under rocks or in well-drained rubble. Without such refuge, they may leave your garden.

Centipedes
Class: Chilopoda

The closest relatives of true insects, centipedes as a group are mostly beneficial. They differ from insects in having no wings or thorax, and they have, as their name implies, many legs. However, they have only one pair of legs per body segment, not 100 legs.

This species, <u>Scutigera coleoptrata</u>, or the house centipede, is often found indoors, but in the southern United States and Europe it can be found in the garden, reducing pest populations!

They run very fast.

Centipedes eat a variety of insects, spiders and snails.

average

size: 1"

Centipedes have poisonous claws on the first body segment behind the head. They use these to subdue their prey.

Large centipedes native to the South and the tropics can inflict a painful bite to humans!

Centipedes are commonly found under logs or boards in moist soil

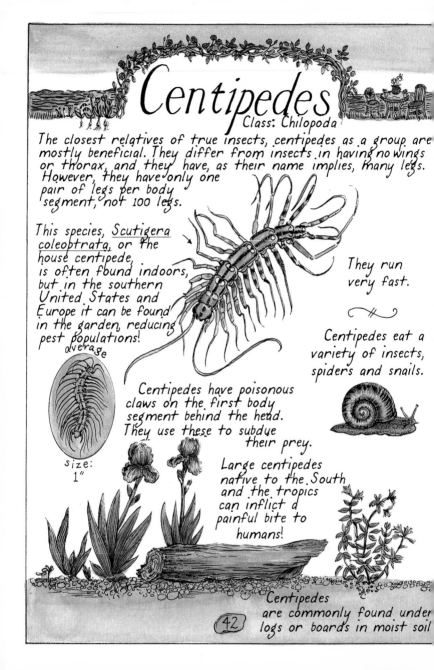

Earthworms

Phylum: Annelida

Aristotle called worms "intestines of the earth" and Darwin said they were "earth's plow."

They can eat their weight in decaying plant matter each day!

his thickened ortion holds the orm's reproductive gans. During mating, o earthworms simulaneously impregnate d become Impregated by each other.

ffspring can live for to 12 years, provided ey aren't found by a ngry bird, a gardener's ade or pesticides the soil.

← actual size

I have countless red wigglers in my compost bin breaking up my kitchen waste and garden clippings

Their tunneling and castings (earthworm poop) help to aerate soil and greatly improve its structure and mineral content. Castings are high in phosphorous, nitrogen and potassium.

Unfortunately, simply adding earthworms to poor soil won't do much good. However, if you add organic material to your soil, chances are the worms will come. Night crawlers half-emerge from their burrows when it is dark and reach around for decaying plant matter to drag down and eat.

Night crawlers' average size: 7"

Nematodes

Phylum: Nematoda

Nasty nematodes attack plant roots, but beneficial nematodes attack soil-borne pests. These tiny roundworms kill their hosts by invading them and then releasing bacteria that cause blood poisoning.

They are microscopic.

They are sold in a paste form—just add water and then sprinkle on moistened soil around plants in the late afternoon or evening.

Scientists are discovering new species that eat different pests every day.

The species called _Steinernema carpocapsea_ is especially effective against caterpillars, cutworms, webworms and billbugs. _Heterorhabditis bacteriophora_ loves Japanese beetle grubs.

Nematodes can also be used to control fleas, iris borers, cabbage root maggots and strawberry root weevils. What a champ!

Glossary

Abdomen. The hindmost of the three major body parts of insects.
Antenna. (*pl.* antennae). Feelerlike sensory appendages on both sides of an insect's head, located above the mouth parts.
Aphid mummies. The tan or black, swollen shells of parasitized aphids, which are found stuck to leaves.
Arthropoda. The phylum of invertebrate animals with an exoskeleton, jointed legs, and segmented bodies, called arthropods. It includes insects, spiders, and mites.
Arthropods. Members of the phylum Arthropoda.
Beak. The protruding mouth parts of an insect, used for sucking.
Caterpillar. The larva of a moth or butterfly.
Class. A subdivision of a phylum or subphylum, made up of a group of related orders.
Cocoon. A case produced by a larva inside which the pupa develops.
Compound eye. An eye made up of many individual parts or facets.
Elytron. (*pl.* elytra). The thickened, leathery front wings of beetles and some other insects.
Family. A subdivision of an order, made up of related genera.

Genus. (*pl.* genera). A group of closely related species; the capitalized first portion of a scientific name.

Grub. The slow-moving, sluggish larva of a beetle.

Head. The first or anterior third of an insect body, where the eyes, antennae, and jaws are located.

Honeydew. A sugary liquid excreted by some insects, especially aphids, scales, mealybugs, and whiteflies.

Host. A plant or animal on or in which a parasitoid lives.

Insecticide. A substance used to kill insects.

Instar. A growth stage of an immature insect.

Larva. (*pl.* larvae). The immature stage, between egg and pupa, of an insect that goes through complete metamorphosis. Differs greatly in appearance from the adult.

Maggot. The legless, wormlike larva of a fly or wasp.

Mandible. A jaw.

Metamorphosis. A change in body form from immature to adult insect.

Mulch. A thick layer of organic matter such as wood chips, grass clippings, compost, or straw that aids in water retention and weed reduction and as a refuge for some insects and animals.

Nymph. The young of an insect that goes through gradual metamorphosis.

Order. A subdivision of a class, made up of related families.

Ovipositor. An egg-depositing organ of female insects located at the end of the abdomen.

Parasite. An organism that spends at least one stage of its life in or on another organism (the host), feeding on the host's body but not necessarily killing it.

Parasitoid. An organism that lives in or on another organism (the host), consuming the host and eventually killing it.

Perennials. Nonwoody plants that live year after year.

Pesticide. A substance used to kill pests, usually insects.

Phylum. A major division of the animal kingdom.

46

Pollen.   The powdery grains produced by the male organs of flowers (anthers).

Pollination.   The process by which pollen is transferred to the stigma (female organ) of a flower, facilitating the plant's reproduction.

Predator.   An animal that eats other animals.

Prey.   The animal a predator hunts.

Pupa. (*pl.* pupae).   The largely inactive developmental stage that occurs between the larval and adult stages in insects undergoing complete metamorphosis.

Pupate.   To become a pupa.

Segment.   A body or appendage subdivision.

Species.   A group of individual insects that share common structures and characteristics and that are able to interbreed and create fertile offspring.

Spurious vein.   A false vein or thickening between two true veins on the wing of an insect.

Suborder.   A subdivision of an order, made up of related families.

Tarsus.   The "foot" portion of the insect leg.

Thorax.   The middle section of an insect's body, located between the head and the abdomen, that carries the legs and wings.

True bugs.   The word *bug* is often used to describe all insects, when in fact only the members of the order Hemiptera are actually bugs. Therefore, "true bugs" describes this order.

References

Borror, D. J., and D. M. DeLong, 1989. *An Introduction to the Study of Insects,* 6th ed. Fort Worth: Harcourt Brace Jovanovich.

Borror, D. J., and R. E. White, 1970. *A Field Guide to the Insects of America North of Mexico.* Boston: Houghton Mifflin.

Callahan, Phillip S. 1970. *Insect Behavior.* New York: Four Winds Press.

Conniff, Richard. July 1993. "On the lowly worm we earthlings pin our loftiest dreams." *Smithsonian,* 86–95.

Cook, Jack. May/June 1991. "Nature's Own Pest Control: Beneficial Insects." *Organic Gardening,* 36–40.

Evans, Howard Ensign. 1985. *The Pleasure of Entomology.* Washington, D.C.: Smithsonian Institution Press.

Flint, M. L. 1990. *Pests of the Garden and Small Farm: A Grower's Guide to Using Less Pesticide.* University of California, Division of Agriculture and Natural Resources, publication no. 3332.

Gilkeson, Linda, and Joel Grossman. May/June 1991. "The Organic Gardening Guide to Important Beneficial Insects and Mites of North America." *Organic Gardening,* 46–54.

Grossman, Joel. November/December 1991. "Stopping Slugs and Snails." *Fine Gardening,* 56–59.

Hoffmann, Michael P., and Anne C. Frodsham. 1993. *Natural Enemies of Vegetable Insect Pests.* Ithaca, N.Y.: Cornell Cooperative Extension.

Hogue, Charles L. 1974. *The Insects of the Los Angeles Basin.* Los Angeles: Natural History Museum of Los Angeles County.

Hunter, Charles D. 1992. *Suppliers of Beneficial Organisms in North America.* Sacramento: California Environmental Protection Agency.

Hutchins, Ross E. 1966. *Insects.* Englewood Cliffs, N.J.: Prentice-Hall.

McGavin, George C. 1992. *American Nature Guides Insects.* New York: Smithmark.

Metcalf, C. L., W. P. Flint, and R. L. Metcalf. 1951. *Destructive and Useful Insects.* New York: McGraw-Hill.

Milne, Lorus, and Margery Milne. 1980. *The Audubon Society Field Guide to North American Insects and Spiders.* New York: Knopf.

Olkowski, William, Sheila Daar, and Helga Olkowski. 1991. *Common-Sense Pest Control.* Newtown, Conn.: Taunton Press.

Poncavage, Joanna. May/June 1991. "Beneficial Borders." *Organic Gardening,* 42–45.

Powell, Jerry A., and Charles L. Hogue. 1979. *California Insects.* Berkeley: University of California Press.

Raver, Anne. May 8, 1994. "Garden Pests? To a Nematode, They're Lunch." *New York Times,* 19.

Rupp, Rebecca. July/August 1992. "The Earthworms." *Country Journal,* 52.

Stoetzel, M. B. 1989. *Common Names of Insects and Related Organisms.* Entomological Society of America.

Stokes, Donald W. 1983. *A Guide to Observing Insect Lives.* Boston: Little, Brown.

Westcott, Cynthia. 1973. *The Gardener's Bug Book.* Garden City, N.Y.: Doubleday.

Yepsen, R. B., Jr., ed. 1984. *The Encyclopedia of Natural Insect and Disease Control.* Emmaus, Penn.: Rodale Press.

Retail Sources

Here is a select list of sources for many of the insects described in this book. Call or write for catalog information or lists of available species.

ARBICO, Inc.
P.O. Box 4247
Tucson, Ariz. 85738
(602) 825-9785

Beneficial Insectary
14751 Oak Run Rd.
Oak Run, Calif. 96069
(916) 472-3715

Biofac
P.O. Box 87
Mathis, Tex. 78368
(512) 547-3259

Bozeman Bio-Tech
1612 Gold Ave.
P.O. Box 3146
Bozeman, Mont. 59772
(406) 587-5891

Gardens Alive!
5100 Schenley
Lawrenceburg, Ind. 47025
(812) 537-8650

Harmony Farm Supply
P.O. Box 460
Graton, Calif. 95444
(707) 823-9125

IFM
333 Ohme Gardens Rd.
Wenatchee, Wash. 98801
(509) 662-3179

Peaceful Valley Farm Supply
P.O. Box 2209
Grass Valley, Calif. 95945
(916) 272-4769

IPM Laboratories, Inc.
Main St.
Locke, N.Y. 13092
(315) 497-2063

Rincon-Vitova Insectaries, Inc.
P.O. Box 1555
Ventura, Calif. 93002
(805) 643-5407

To order a more comprehensive list of retail sources, *Suppliers of Beneficial Organisms in North America* by Charles D. Hunter, write to:

Department of Pesticide Regulation
Environmental Monitoring and Pest Management Branch
1020 N St.
Sacramento, Calif. 94271
(916) 324-4100

The following catalogs offer bulbs, tools, stepping stones, seeds, and everything else to help you create an ideal habitat for beneficial insects:

Brookstone
1655 Bassford Drive
Mexico, Mo. 65265
(800) 846-3000

Gardener's Eden
P.O. Box 7307
San Francisco, Calif. 94120
(800) 822-1214

Clapper's
1125 Washington St.
West Newton, Mass. 02165
(617) 244-7900

Gardener's Supply
128 Intervale Rd.
Burlington, Vt. 05401
(802) 863-1700

Smith & Hawken
25 Corte Madera Ave.
Mill Valley, Calif. 94941
(800) 776-5558

David Kay
One Jenni Lane
Peoria, Ill. 61614
(707) 585-9811
(800) 535-9917

Plow & Hearth
301 Madison Rd.
Orange, Va. 22960
(800) 866-8072

Wayside Gardens
1 Garden Lane
Hodges, S.C. 29695
(800) 845-1124

Index